JOHN CHARLES FRÉMONT

Pathfinder to the West

HAROLD FABER

BENCHMARK BOOKS

MARSHALL CAVENDISH
NEW YORK

With special thanks to Professor Steven Pitti, Yale University,
for his careful reading of this manuscript.

Benchmark Books
Marshall Cavendish
99 White Plains Road
Tarrytown, New York 10591-9001

Library of Congress Cataloging-in-Publication Data

Faber, Harold.
    John Charles Frémont: pathfinder to the West / by Harold Faber.
        p.cm – (Great explorations)
Summary: A biography of the nineteenth-century soldier, politician, and explorer whose many
expeditions helped open up the American West to settlers.
Includes bibliographical references (p.) and index.
ISBN 0-7614-1481-9
1. Frémont, John Charles, 1813-1890—Juvenile literature. 2 Explorers—West (U.S.)—
Biographpy—Juvenile literature. 3. Explorers—United States—Biography—Juvenile literature.
4. West (U.S.)—Discovery and exploration—Juvenile literature. 5. Presidential candidates—
United States—Biography—Juvenile literature. 6. Generals—United States—Biography—Juvenile
literature. [1. Frémont, John Charles, 1813-1890. 2. Explorers. 3. West (U.S.)—Discovery and
exploration.] I. Title: John Charles Frémont, pathfinder to the West. II. Title. III. Series.

E415.9.F8 F33 2002
979'.02'092—dc21
[B]   2002018461

Photo Research by Candlepants Incorporated
Cover Photo: Smithsonian American Art Museum, Wasington, DC / Art Resource
Cover Photo (top): Corbis/Bettman
The photographs in this book are used by permission and through the courtesy of:
Western History Collection, Denver Public Library: 5, 26; *Art Resource, NY*: National Portrait Gallery, Washington,
D.C., 7, 41, 53; Smithsonian American Art Museum, 57; Reunion des Musees Nationaux, 62. *South Carolina
Historical Society*: 9. Corbis: Dave G. Houser, 10, 23; Bettman, 33; Archivo Iconographico S.A., 69; *Army Art
Collection, U.S. Army Center for Military History*: 11. *Minnesota Historical Society*: 15, 25, 49; *Bancroft Library,
University of California, Berkley*: 16, 24, 34, 36, 38, 42, 46, 50, 59, 60, 65; *The Southwest Museum, Los Angeles*:
(#81.G.2) 18, (Schenck & Schenck #04-2000) 31; *Western History Collection, University of Oklahoma*: 29, 37;
California History Section, California State Library: 45; *Henry E. Huntington Library and Art Gallery*: 73

Printed in Hong Kong

1   3   5   6   4   2

Contents

foreword

In his time, John Charles Frémont was one of the best-known explorers of the United States. Although he was not the first to venture into the vast wilderness of the American West, he explored more of it than any other man. His reports about practical paths through the mountains and deserts of the West inspired thousands of pioneers to follow in his footsteps seeking new lives in California, Oregon, and Washington.

As an explorer, mapmaker, writer, soldier, and politician, he became famous—and controversial. In a roller-coaster career, he played a major part in establishing California as a state, but then was convicted by an army court-martial on charges of mutiny. Despite that disgrace, he remained so popular in 1856, that the new Republican Party chose him as its first candidate for president. After he lost, he fell back into relative obscurity.

John Charles Frémont commanded the Western Department of the Union Army during the Civil War, but his rash political actions forced President Abraham Lincoln to remove him from the position.

Once more, at the beginning of the Civil War, he emerged in a high position, but not for long. In 1862, President Lincoln appointed him a major general commanding a Union army in the West, but soon thereafter he was dismissed because he prematurely freed slaves in Missouri.

What kind of man could rise from obscurity to fame and then fall into failure, to rise from poverty to riches and then drop back into poverty? Was he the victim of the partisan politics of his day, or did he contain within himself the seeds of his own destruction?

Today, more than a hundred years after his death, Frémont's political and military mistakes are largely forgotten, and he is remembered for his major achievements as the "pathfinder to the West."

O N E

The Making of an Explorer

John Charles Frémont was born in Savannah, Georgia, on January 21, 1813. His parents were Anne Whiting Pryor, the daughter of a well-known Virginia family, and Charles Frémon, who had fled from France to America during the French Revolution of 1789.

After arriving in the United States, Frémon, a charming and handsome man, made his living as a teacher of French and dance in Richmond, Virginia. One of his pupils was Mrs. Pryor, the unhappy young wife of Major John Pryor, an elderly and ailing landowner. She and Frémon fell in love and ran away together in 1811, but could not get married because Pryor was still alive. Frémon died when John was still very young.

Young John—whom his mother called Charley—grew up in Charleston, South Carolina. His mother took in boarders to support herself and her children. Charley, the oldest, had a younger sister, Elizabeth, who died as a child, and a younger brother, Frank, who died in an accident as a young man.

John Charles Frémont was known as a brash young man, and in 1831
he was expelled from college for irregular attendance.

Charley was a good student. He did so well in his studies that his mother thought that he might become a minister or a lawyer. When he turned fourteen, Charley's mother arranged for him to work as a clerk in the law office of John W. Mitchell, a friend of the family. He paid for Charley to attend a preparatory school for Charleston College.

A good-looking, active boy with curly black hair, Charley attended the school for two years, from 1827 to 1829. Dr. Charles Robertson, the headmaster, described him as "of middle size, graceful in manners, rather slender, but well formed, and upon the whole what I would call handsome, of a keen piercing eye, and a noble forehead." What impressed Dr. Robertson the most, however, was how quickly Charley learned the ancient languages of Greek and Latin.

After two years of study under Dr. Robertson, Charley entered Charleston College. Although he started out deficient in mathematics, he made up for it with his quick mind and attention to his studies. "At sixteen, I was a good scholar," he remembered proudly in his memoirs.

Then suddenly, he began to miss some of his classes. The reason? He had fallen in love with a beautiful young girl named Cecelia. She and her family were refugees from a war on the Caribbean island of Hispaniola. When he met her, the romantic, young Charley forgot about his studies.

Charley ignored the school's warnings about failing his courses. In 1831, just three months short of graduating, he was dismissed for what the college called "habitual irregularity and incorrigible negligence." Later, in his memoirs, he remembered:

I smiled to myself while I listened to the words about disappointment of friends—and the broken career. I was living in a charmed atmosphere and their edict only gave me complete freedom. What the poets dwell on as the rarest flower of life had blossomed in my path—only seventeen, I was passionately in love.

Charleston Academy, the college Frémont attended

But his joy did not last long. Like many teenage romances, that of Charley and Cecelia began to fade, and finally ended. Back in the real world, Charley faced the necessity of earning a living. He found a job teaching in a private school in Charleston. Several years later, he added a *t* to his last name and became known as John Charles Frémont.

For the next ten years, Frémont learned the basics of being an explorer.

His apprenticeship started in the home of Joel Roberts Poinsett, who had just returned to Charleston after serving as the United States' minister to Mexico. As a bright, educated young man, Frémont was invited to attend weekly breakfasts that Poinsett held for the leaders of Charleston society and distinguished visitors. There, Frémont heard stories of travel and adventure and decided that he, too, would like to venture forth to distant places.

9

THE POINSETTIA

Joel Roberts Poinsett (1779–1851) is remembered today for a plant, the poinsettia, which is named after him. His fame dates to 1829, when he returned from Mexico with a lovely plant that prospered in greenhouses. His career as the United States' first minister to Mexico and secretary of war in the cabinet of President Martin Van Buren, however, has been largely for-

gotten. Today, the poinsettia, with leaves of bright red and dark green—the colors of Christmas—is widely used as an indoor holiday decoration all over the country.

Poinsett, who had influence in Washington, helped Frémont obtain a position as a teacher of mathematics on a navy ship, the Natchez, then in Charleston. In those days, before the establishment of the United States Naval Academy at Annapolis in 1845, young cadets received their education aboard naval vessels.

In 1833, Frémont sailed aboard the Natchez to various ports in South America. For him, it was the equivalent of the completion of his college courses—reading in the ship's library, visiting strange cities, and making new friends among the junior naval officers. Two years later, in 1835, the trip was over, and Frémont was back in Charleston, unemployed.

Offered a position as a professor of mathematics in the navy, he

The Making of an Explorer

Joel Roberts Poinsett was appointed the first American minister to Mexico in 1825.

turned it down for a more appealing job. He became an assistant in a land survey of a route for a railroad between Charleston and Cincinnati. The survey ended in the fall, and Frémont was unemployed once again.

But not for long. The army was called upon to make a survey of the mountainous region where the states of North Carolina, Tennessee, and Georgia came together—the home of the Cherokee Indians. The government had decided to move the Cherokee farther west, opening up the land to white settlers, and needed maps to show in detail the area involved. Frémont was asked to become an assistant on the survey team.

In the autumn and winter of 1836 and 1837, Frémont and the others went out into a heavily forested area to make their maps. He learned how to live in the wilderness, including how to find food; properly pack a mule with food, tools, and cooking utensils; set up a tent in a snowdrift; build a fire in the snows and winds of winter; and make meals of flour, water, and raw meat. He later wrote:

> *Here I found the path on which I was destined to walk. Through many of the years to come the occupation of my prime of life was to be among Indians and in waste places.*

T W O

The Way West and Romance

Frémont's education as an explorer took a new direction in 1838, when he was assigned to a mapping mission west of the Mississippi River.

In Washington, Poinsett, now secretary of war, decided that the army needed maps of the area between the Mississippi and Missouri Rivers. Following his orders, the army's Topographical Corps of Engineers hired an eminent French scientist living in the United States, Joseph Nicholas Nicollet, to make the survey.

Nicollet had imposing credentials. A skilled astronomer and mapmaker, he was a member of the French Legion of Honor. He had come to the United States in 1832 and had already explored the upper Mississippi River.

Now fifty-two years old, Nicollet needed a young, vigorous assistant, one with some experience in surveying, mathematics, and the wilderness. Frémont met the requirements perfectly. Poinsett recom-

J. N. Nicollet
Philadelphia May 8th 1843.

A silhouette of eminent French astronomer and mathematician Joseph Nicholas Nicollet

mended him for an appointment as a second lieutenant in the Topographical Corps, and Frémont was ordered to St. Louis to meet Nicollet.

In St. Louis, Frémont was responsible for getting the necessary supplies for the expedition. With the help of Pierre Chouteau, a leading fur trader, he bought barometers, chronometers, microscopes, thermometers, compasses, paper, ink, pens, and pencils for observations; dried beef, pork in barrels, ham, bacon, flour, salt, butter, rice, potatoes, sugar, tea, and coffee for food; plates, knives and forks, and cups for eating; blankets, mosquito netting, lanterns, candles, soap, and a medicine chest for comfort; rifles and ammunition for protection; and knives and cloth as presents for the Indians they might meet.

That done, Frémont, Nicollet, and their men left in May 1838 on a river steamboat up the Mississippi River. Their destination was Fort Snelling, five hundred miles upriver, where the Minnesota River meets the Mississippi.

They camped at a nearby trading post of the American Fur Company. The manager, Henry Sibley, furnished the expedition with several two-wheeled carts, each pulled by a horse, for the trip by land along the banks of the Minnesota River to the northwest.

With the snows of winter coming soon, the expedition ended its

---

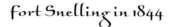

Fort Snelling in 1844

The waterfront of St. Louis, as seen from the Mississippi River, 1836

---

first session of observations and returned to St. Louis. Nicollet dispatched Frémont to Washington to make a report to Poinsett. Frémont returned to St. Louis in the spring of 1839, ready to join the party on the second half of the mapping project.

On April 4, 1839, they left St. Louis on a river steamboat for a long trip up the Missouri River, traveling the same route that Lewis and Clark had followed some thirty-five years before. Many years later, in his memoirs, Frémont recalled their arrival:

At length, on the seventieth day, we reached Fort Pierre, the chief post of the American Fur Company. This is on the right or western bank of the river, about one thousand and three hundred miles from St. Louis. On the prairie, a few miles away was a large village of Yankton Sioux. Here we were in the heart of Indian country and near the great buffalo ranges. Here the Indians were sovereign.

After hiring additional scouts and hunters, Nicollet's party left Fort Pierre. On horseback, they traveled northeast toward the Canadian border, over a level plain covered with grass and wildflowers. Frémont was overwhelmed by the beauty of the area. But the most exciting spectacle was his first sight of a huge herd of buffalo. "This was an event on which my imagination had been dwelling," he said. The great mass of animals, grazing as they moved south to their wintering quarters and

A buffalo hunt

covering the landscape as far as the eye could see, impressed him deeply.

Making observations of latitude and longitude as it went, the expedition moved north to Devil's Lake, not far from the Canadian border, and then turned south. As night was falling on a November day, Frémont, with a small detachment of men in canoes, reached Prairie du Chien, in what is today western Wisconsin. There he learned another hard lesson of exploration, as he explained in his memoirs:

> *A steamboat on the landing was firing up and just about starting for St. Louis, but we thought it would be pleasant to rest a day or two and enjoy comfortable quarters while waiting for the next boat. But the next boat was in the spring, for next morning it was snowing hard, and the river was frozen from bank to bank. I had enough time while there to learn two valuable things: one, how to skate; the other, the value of a day.*

Frémont returned to Washington at the end of 1839—and his life changed dramatically.

After Nicollet and Frémont reported to President Martin Van Buren, they settled down to the careful work of translating their notes and sketches into maps. In his memoirs, Frémont explained why map-making was a long and complicated process:

> *First, the foundations must be laid in observations in the field; then the reduction of those observations to latitude and longitude; afterward the projection of the map, and the laying down upon it of positions fixed by the observations; then the tracing from the sketchbooks of the lines of the rivers, the forms of the lakes, the contours of the hills . . . fixing on a small sheet of paper the results of laborious travel over waste regions, and giving to them an enduring place on the world's surface.*

Many government officials visited to see how the mapmaking was progressing. Among them was Thomas Hart Benton, the senior senator from Missouri, a strong supporter of exploring the lands beyond the Mississippi River. Frémont was welcomed warmly by Benton and his wife and joined them for dinner night after night. The Bentons had three children at home—two daughters, Susan and Eliza, and one son, Randolph—and two more daughters, Jessie and Sarah, in school in nearby Georgetown. Frémont first met Jessie at a school concert.

Jessie was more than just a beautiful girl, with sparkling brown eyes, brown hair, and an oval face. She sparkled in conversation, she was good-humored and witty, familiar with all the politicians who came to consult her father, and keenly interested in books.

Jessie Hart Benton was well-known in Washington. She had access to many powerful politicians.

Despite the difference in their ages—she was not quite sixteen and he was twenty-seven—it was love at first sight. Frémont said, "There came a glow into my heart which changed the current and color of daily life and gave beauty to common things."

To Jessie, Frémont was a romantic, handsome young man, with an attractive shy manner. At five foot nine, Frémont was not tall, but his curly dark brown hair was appealing. He was soft-spoken and quiet, but when he did speak, he told stories about his adventures in the mapping expedition, all of which lent him a dashing air.

Senator and Mrs. Benton were not pleased at the budding romance. They thought that Jessie was much too young for marriage, and that Frémont, as much as they liked him, was poor, with little prospect for promotion in the army. They insisted that the young couple wait a year. If at the end of that period they were still in love, they could get married.

Mrs. Benton took another step to separate them. She spoke to her friend Mrs. Poinsett, who talked to her husband, the secretary of war. Suddenly, Frémont received orders to proceed immediately to survey the Des Moines River in the Iowa Territory.

As an army officer, Frémont obeyed. In early July, he was on the Des Moines River, traveling by canoe, making observations, noting the fine soil along its banks suitable for farming, taking astronomical readings, and sketching changes in the course of the river. He completed the survey quickly, returning to Washington—and to Jessie—in early September.

The young lovers decided that they wanted to get married immediately. But there was a problem. None of the Protestant ministers they approached were willing to perform the marriage ceremony, because Jessie was not yet eighteen years old and they feared the wrath of her powerful father. Finally, a friend convinced a Catholic priest to perform the ceremony, and they were married on October 19, 1841.

She returned to her home and Frémont to his quarters, keeping the

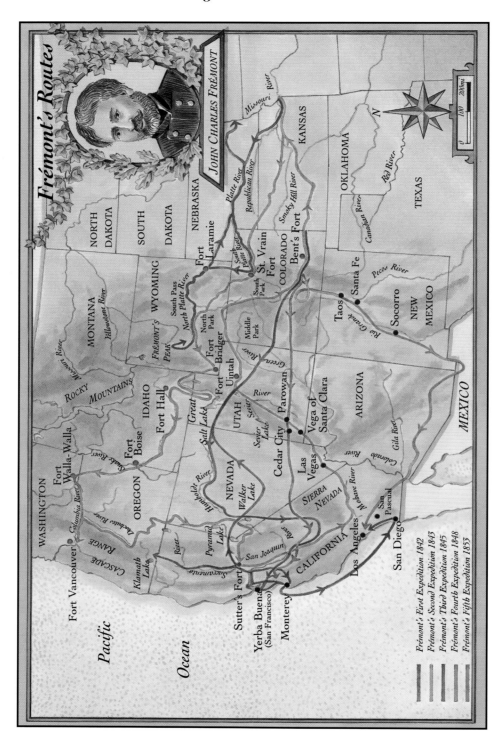

Frémont's Routes

JOHN CHARLES FRÉMONT

Frémont's First Expedition 1842
Frémont's Second Expedition 1843
Frémont's Third Expedition 1845
Frémont's Fourth Expedition 1848
Frémont's Fifth Expedition 1853

marriage a secret until they found the right moment to tell her parents. In early November, they faced her father.

"Get out of my house and never cross my door again! Jessie shall stay here," Benton said angrily.

Jessie clutched her husband's arm. "Whither thou goest, I will go, and where thou lodgest, I will lodge: thy people shall be my people, and thy God my God," she said, quoting the words of Ruth in the Bible.

Benton knew when he was defeated. Faced with the choice of losing his daughter or accepting his new son-in-law, he made a decision.

"Go collect your belongings and return at once to the house. I will prepare Mrs. Benton," he told Frémont. After Frémont did so, the Benton home became the home of the newlyweds, too.

That welcome marked two great changes in Frémont's life—the beginning of a happy marriage and of a great career as an independent explorer, backed by his father-in-law—one of the most powerful senators in Washington.

The routes of Frémont's five expeditions to the West

T H R E E

The First Expedition

In 1842, the leaders of the United States government saw the West as the natural region for the geographical growth of the country. Back then, the United States extended about two-thirds of the way from the Atlantic Ocean to the Pacific. Beyond its borders was land that was not yet part of the country, including:

• The Republic of Texas, which had achieved independence from Mexico in 1836 but was not yet a state
• California, which included not only the present state of California itself but also Nevada, Utah, Arizona, New Mexico, and parts of Colorado and Wyoming, all owned by Mexico
• The disputed territory of Oregon, which included the present states of Oregon, Washington, and Idaho, and parts of Wyoming and Montana, claimed by Great Britain

The First Expedition

That vast land west of the Mississippi River was largely unknown territory to most Americans living in the East. They knew, of course, that it was populated by many different Indian tribes, but Indian rights were of no concern to them. They had little knowledge of its geography—its mountains, rivers, prairies, and deserts.

Some information came from trappers, hunters, and traders who had ventured in to harvest beaver pelts along the mountain streams for sale in Europe, where they were in great demand for hats and coats. Some of these bold adventurers became known as "mountain men," because they knew how to travel safely in the wilderness. Their knowledge was all in their heads, however.

In addition, there were several reports from army expeditions. The most notable was that of Meriwether Lewis and William Clark, who

---

The Oregon Trail, as drawn by Charles Preuss

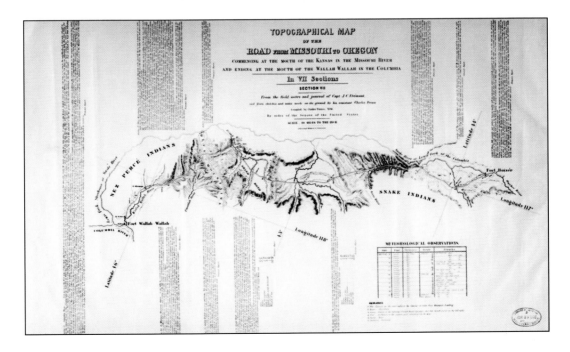

traveled the length of the Missouri River and crossed the mountains to the Pacific Ocean from 1804 to 1806. Their maps were excellent, but their difficult route was obviously not suited for emigrant families.

Three other army expeditions produced information, but no usable maps. In 1806, Lieutenant Zebulon M. Pike had traveled to Santa Fe, Major Stephen H. Long had reached the Rocky Mountains in 1820, and Captain Benjamin deBonneville from 1832 to 1835 had explored the area around the Great Salt Lake in Utah.

What the country needed was detailed maps, if large numbers of emigrants were to move into the area. Nicollet, the expert mapmaker, was too old and sick to do the job. The obvious next choice was his assistant, Frémont. He was young, active, brave, experienced—and he had the backing of the American most interested in mapping the West, his father-in-law, Senator Benton.

Starting Point

The starting point for all of Frémont's expeditions and for emigrants to Oregon and California was near what is now Kansas City, Missouri. Some expeditions left from Independence, a suburb of Kansas City, on the east bank of the Missouri River. But most started from across the Missouri River, at a small settlement at the junction of the Kansas River variously called Kaw Landing or Kanzas, or Westport or Westport Landing.

From there, the route was directly west a short distance, before it broke into two. The Santa Fe Trail dipped southwest to Colorado and New Mexico, while the Oregon Trail went northwest into Nebraska and then west along the Great Platte River Road to South Pass in Wyoming and through the mountains to the Pacific Ocean.

Westport landing, a starting point for travelers to the West

Frémont received orders to explore and map the country between the Missouri River and the Rocky Mountains. On May 2, 1842, he left Washington, leaving behind his bride of six months.

With him, he had an assistant, Charles Preuss, an experienced mapmaker, and his young brother-in-law, Randolph Benton, then only twelve years old. In St. Louis, Frémont hired twenty-one men experienced in traveling and hunting in the West. He also agreed to take along

Henry Brant, the nineteen-year-old son of his host in St. Louis. All he needed was an experienced guide.

Frémont boarded a steamboat for the trip up the Missouri River to western Missouri, the jumping-off place for the expedition. By coincidence, aboard the boat Frémont met the man who not only would be his guide, but who became a lifelong companion, friend, and supporter, Christopher "Kit" Carson.

Carson (1809–1868) was a man of few words, but he possessed vast experience in the West. At that time, "no one was better skilled in Indian customs and ways and mental habits, and no one knew more of the craft of the mountains and the plains," according to one Frémont biographer. Frémont liked Carson immediately, and hired him.

Kit Carson standing at left; Frémont sitting at right

The First Expedition

On June 10, 1842, Frémont left, leading a column of men armed with rifles and mounted on horses. They followed the Santa Fe Trail for a while, but then turned northwest until they reached the Platte River in what is now Nebraska.

Frémont immediately established the rules of the march. Each night, an hour before sunset, they would stop, wheel their supply carts into a compact circle for protection, pitch tents, set fires to prepare supper, and get to sleep by nine o'clock. They would awaken each morning at four-thirty, and be on the march again at six-thirty. Frémont himself was busy from morning to midnight. Twice a day he took astronomical observations. He also wrote a detailed daily journal, noting the botanical and geological features of the country. In addition to that, he made maps.

On July 9, Frémont caught his first glimpse of the Rocky Mountains, some sixty miles away. A week later, he arrived at Fort Laramie, just inside the eastern border of the present state of Wyoming. Despite its name, Fort Laramie was not an army post, but a trading outpost of the American Fur Company.

There, Frémont received bad news—the Sioux and other Indians were at war with each other west of Fort Laramie, which meant that any movement toward South Pass was dangerous. His trusted aide, Kit Carson, warned him against proceeding further.

For five days, Frémont considered his options. To turn back would mean failure—failure to reach the goal of the expedition. To go on meant risking the lives of his men. As a soldier, Frémont made the bold decision to go forward. But he took some precautions. He hired an interpreter to talk to any Sioux he might meet, and he left the two boys, Randolph Benton and Henry Brant, behind for safekeeping.

On July 21, Frémont and his well-armed men left Fort Laramie, moving west cautiously. They left the Platte River trail and followed the Sweetwater River west. They met a few Indians along the way, but none of them proved hostile.

KIT CARSON

Christopher "Kit" Carson was born in Kentucky in 1809. At the age of fifteen, he ran away from his boring job as an apprentice to a saddle maker to join an expedition to Santa Fe, New Mexico. It was the beginning of an exciting new life for Kit, who in a few years became famous as a "mountain man"—someone who knew how to survive and thrive in the hostile wilderness that then was the West.

Soft-spoken and mild-mannered, Carson was a skilled hunter and trapper, a wise guide, a fierce fighter when necessary, and a loyal and true friend. Although he could not read or write, he mastered the art of living in the mountains, deserts, and plains of the West; no one was better acquainted with Indian life, customs, and habits.

With all those skills, he was an invaluable addition to Frémont's expeditions, admired by all who met him. "A braver man than Kit perhaps never lived," one army officer said. Frémont himself said, "With me Carson and Truth mean the same thing. He is always the same—gallant and disinterested."

When the expeditions ended, Carson retired to his ranch in Taos, New Mexico. Because of his knowledge of the Indians, he was appointed a United States agent in charge of relations with the Indian tribes in New Mexico. When the Civil War broke out, he organized and commanded the First New Mexico Volunteers, serving on the western frontier, with the rank of colonel in the Union army. For gallantry in battle against hostile Indian forces, he was promoted to brigadier general. He died in 1868.

Fort Laramie, Wyoming

On August 8, they reached South Pass, in what is today southwestern Wyoming. South Pass was (and is) more than a mile high, at 7,550 feet (2,300 meters), about 950 miles (1,530 kilometers) from where Frémont had started in Kansas.

The sight of South Pass was a big surprise to Frémont. Instead of being a narrow gap in the mountains, it was a broad, sandy opening across the Continental Divide, wide enough for horse- or mule-drawn wagons to pass through, and thus a natural route for emigrant families. The Continental Divide marked the point at which rivers on one side flowed east to the Mississippi River, and on the other side, west to the Pacific Ocean.

With the first part of his mission completed, Frémont turned to exploring the Wind River Range, a chain of mountains northwest of South Pass. In contrast to the easy approach to South Pass, climbing the rugged Wind River Range, the highest mountains in Wyoming, was

REPORT TO THE NATION

After completing his first epedition, Frémont's next task was to write a report of his journey, but he found he just could not write. His wife came up with the solution. He would dictate, and Jessie would take down his words. For months, from nine o'clock in the morning until one o'clock in the afternoon, she sat at her desk, writing, while he paced around the room, notes in his hand, and talked about his adventures.

It turned out to be a great story. Not only did it give full and precise information about the way west, but it also told exciting anecdotes about the animals and Indians that he met. Published by Congress in March 1843, together with maps, it became a valuable book for emigrants. It also established Frémont's reputation as an explorer.

difficult. On August 15, Frémont worked his way across jagged rocks to the highest peaks. He recalled what happened next in his memoirs:

> *I sprang upon the summit, and another step would have precipitated me into an immense snow-field five hundred feet below. To the edge of this field was a sheer icy precipice; and then with a gradual fall, the field sloped off for a mile . . . I stood on a narrow crest, about three feet in width.*

He fixed a pole in a crevice and unfurled an American flag to wave in the breeze. He thought he had reached the top of the highest peak in the Wind River Range, but he was wrong. The mountain he climbed, now called Frémont Peak, is 13,745 feet (4,190 meters) in elevation. A little to the north is Gannett Peak, 13,804 feet (4,200 meters) high.

The expedition returned to Fort Laramie on August 31, forty-two days after it had left, and to St. Louis on October 17. Frémont sped on to Washington, arriving there on October 29, to be reunited with his family. A few days after his arrival, his wife, Jessie, gave birth to their first child, a daughter named Elizabeth and called Lily.

Standing over his wife's bed, Frémont spread out an American flag that he had carried back from his expedition. "This flag was raised over the highest peak of the Rocky Mountains; I have brought it to you," he told her.

The flag that Frémont raised over the Wind River Mountains

$F\ O\ U\ R$

The Second Expedition

Frémont's second expedition might never have happened if not for his wife's forethought. At Westport Landing, in May 1843, Frémont was about to leave on the expedition when he received an urgent letter from Jessie in St. Louis.

"Only trust me and go," the letter said.

The next morning, May 30, Frémont, who had complete confidence in his wife's judgment, left.

Behind that message was a bureaucratic problem. While in St. Louis, Frémont had asked for and received a small cannon to take on his expedition as an added measure of protection. But when army officers heard about it, they questioned the need for a cannon on a mapping expedition. They sent orders for him to stop his preparations and return to Washington with an explanation. When Jessie opened her husband's mail in St. Louis, she acted to protect him by sending him off before the official notification could reach him.

John Charles Frémont, the "Pathfinder," became a national hero early in life for his trailblazing exploits in the far West.

The Second Expedition

Her scheme worked, and the second Frémont expedition began. This time, his objectives were to find a different and easier route to South Pass in Wyoming and then to map a route from the Rocky Mountains to the Pacific Ocean. He hired thirty-nine experienced men, once more including Preuss, the mapmaker.

His most important recruit was Thomas Fitzpatrick, a famous "mountain man" whom he hired as his guide. With a reputation as great as that of Kit Carson, Fitzpatrick was an impressive figure, well known to the Indians as "Broken Hand" because an accident with an exploding rifle had caused the loss of some fingers on one hand.

Instead of following the well-known route to the Platte River, Frémont moved directly west. On July 4, he arrived at St. Vrain's Fort in

---

There were many forts and trading posts along the Columbia River. Here, Fort Vancouver, a British trading post in Canada, is pictured.

northeastern Colorado. A few days later, he met his old friend Kit Carson, who cheerfully joined the expedition.

Day after day, they plodded northwest until they reached South Pass. After a slight detour south to the Great Salt Lake in Utah, Frémont returned in mid-September to the Oregon Trail at Fort Hall, in what is now eastern Idaho. Fort Hall was owned by the Hudson's Bay Company, a British fur trading organization, in territory that was disputed between Great Britain and the United States.

Following the Snake River, Frémont crossed Idaho to Fort Boise, also operated by the British, and then moved northwest across Oregon to the Columbia River, arriving in late October. He had traveled two thousand miles from the Missouri River without any trouble from hostile Indians or any need to use the cannon his men carried.

When he reached the Columbia River, the second part of his mission was accomplished. Instead of going back the way he had come, Frémont decided to explore a largely unknown region to the south—land owned by another country, Mexico. On November 25, 1843, Frémont and twenty-four men left the Columbia River and turned south along the eastern rim of the Cascade Mountains.

On New Year's Day, 1844, they crossed into Mexican territory. On January 10, they reached a large lake in western Nevada that Frémont named Pyramid Lake. A few days later, they camped south of the present site of Reno, Nevada, close to Lake Tahoe.

Here Frémont faced three possible choices: spend the winter comfortably in the valley, resting for the return trip; leave immediately for home across the desert and the Rocky Mountains; or attempt to cross the Sierra Nevada into California, which was then part of Mexico.

Despite warnings by friendly Indians that the Sierras were impassable in the middle of the winter because of high snow and ice, Frémont chose to attempt a crossing. It was a foolhardy decision, placing him and his men in danger that could have been avoided easily. But

Pyramid Lake, named by Frémont

Frémont, then and later, was so confident of his own abilities and decisions that he gave little thought to the possible danger.

On January 19, they started out. Soon, Frémont decided to abandon the small cannon that he had carried all the way from St. Louis. The heavy cannon had proved to be useless.

The warnings of the Indians about snow proved to be correct. It was three to four feet deep and the temperature was frequently below zero. As Frémont reported later:

The snow deepened rapidly, and it soon became necessary to break a road. For this service, a party of ten was formed, mounted on the strongest horses, each man in succession opening the road on foot, or on horseback, until himself and the horse became fatigued, when he stepped aside, and the remaining number passing ahead, he took his station in the rear.

Lack of food was a problem, too. Every day and a half, they killed a horse or a mule for food. They even ate their pet dog.

Day by day, they struggled up the mountains through the deep snowdrifts, sometimes on horseback, sometimes on snowshoes. A less determined man might have thought of turning back. But Frémont was determined and pushed on.

Finally, on February 20, 1844, three months after they started, they reached the pass through the snowcapped mountains, about one and a half miles high. They figured that the elevation was 9,338 feet

---

A pass in the Sierra Nevada Mountains

(2,850 meters), but actually it was 8,634 feet (2,630 meters). They looked down on the beautiful, green Sacramento Valley.

"We now considered ourselves victorious over the mountain," Frémont wrote in his memoirs.

But it took more than two weeks before the half-starved, exhausted group of men made their way, on March 8, to the gates of Sutter's Fort, a prosperous ranch in the valley. Out of the sixty-seven horses and mules that Frémont had when he started the Sierra crossing, only thirty-three survived, so thin that they could hardly walk. Through the generosity of John Augustus Sutter, the owner of the ranch, the men and animals regained their strength.

Two weeks later, Frémont and his men began the long trip home. Once more, instead of going back the way they had come, Frémont decided to go south, following an easy path around the Sierra Nevada and then east—a journey of two thousand miles.

Sutter's Fort, 1847

The Second Expedition

At first, they passed through a beautiful countryside, filled with green pastures and varied flowers. Then they entered the Mojave Desert, a "desolate and revolting country, where lizards were the only animals." There they turned east on the well-known Spanish Trail to Santa Fe, traveling through mostly desert areas.

Instead of going to Santa Fe, though, Frémont chose a route that passed through the southern tip of Nevada into Utah. On familiar ground once more, he traveled across Colorado and Kansas to Westport, where he took a boat down the Missouri River to St. Louis. He arrived on August 6 for a reunion with his wife, fourteen months after he had left.

Together they returned to Washington and lived with Senator Benton and his family. As before, he and Jessie worked together every day on his report. He paced the floor, dictating from his notes, and Jessie dutifully wrote them down.

When Frémont presented his report to the War Department on March 1, 1845, the government ordered ten thousand copies printed. It became a bestseller, eagerly sought by would-be emigrants to California and Oregon because of its precise directions and descriptions of the trail west. Frémont, at the age of thirty-two, became a celebrity.

The army recognized his accomplishment by giving Frémont, who was a second lieutenant, an unusual double promotion to the rank of captain.

FIVE

The Third Expedition: California

James K. Polk was sworn in as president of the United States on March 4, 1845. One of his goals was to acquire California for the United States, even though it was then a province of a foreign country, Mexico.

Frémont soon received orders from Polk to organize another exploratory expedition to the West. Although there was no mention of California in his orders, Frémont clearly understood that he was expected to go there if a war with Mexico broke out.

In June 1845, he arrived in St. Louis, where he recruited fifty-five men. They rode across familiar ground in Missouri and Kansas until they reached Bent's Fort in eastern Colorado on August 2.

But there was one more man that he needed—Kit Carson. He sent a messenger to Carson, who operated a ranch on the Cimarron River, near Taos, New Mexico, asking him to join up. Carson immediately left his ranch and rode to join Frémont.

President James K. Polk

Bent's Fort, Colorado

On August 16, Frémont led a small army of well-armed men out of Bent's Fort. It was "the beginning of two crowded years whose adventures, perils, triumphs and humiliations were to make him one of the most famous figures of his generation," according to historian Allan Nevins.

Early in September, Frémont reached the shores of the Great Salt Lake in Utah. To the west, he faced a major obstacle—a seemingly impassable desert. The local Indians said they knew of no one who had ever crossed it. To Frémont, this was a challenge he could not refuse.

At the far end of the desert, fifty miles or so away, he spotted a peaked, wooded mountain, which indicated that water might be available there. He dispatched Carson and three other men to make a night crossing of the desert, with instructions to make a huge bonfire if they found water.

A day later, when Frémont saw a fire, he and his entire party crossed the desert, too. At the end of the sandy wastes, he found water. His gamble had paid off. He had saved the weeks and miles of travel that it would have taken to detour around the desert. Still another major obstacle on his road to California lay ahead—the Sierra Nevada Mountains, which had proved to be so difficult to cross the year before. With winter snows coming, Frémont made a prudent decision. He divided the expedition in two, sending the main party south to circle around the Sierras. He himself, with only fifteen men, decided to push straight ahead across the mountains.

He was lucky. In that December of 1845, the weather turned mild. Instead of snow, he found relatively balmy conditions. He made the mountain crossing in six days, instead of the six terrible weeks of his previous crossing. On December 9, Frémont arrived once more at Sutter's Fort, in California.

* * *

Frémont and his small army—almost sixty well-armed men—marched into a complicated political situation in California.

At that time, in 1846, California was a province of Mexico, far from its capital of Mexico City. Its small population was divided about seeking independence or becoming part of the United States.

There were three active political groups in the province; a few Mexican officials and troops; several hundred native Mexican citizens who lived in California and wanted to separate it from Mexico they called themselves "Californios"; and about eight hundred American settlers. The largest segment of the population, various Indian tribes numbering about twenty thousand, had no voice in governing and were largely ignored.

As a visitor to a foreign land, Frémont acted properly. He visited Monterey, at that time the capital of California, in March, and reported to the American consul, Thomas Larkin. He paid a call upon the Mexican officials and notified them that he was leading a party of civilians—not soldiers—to make a survey of the shortest route between the United States and the Pacific Ocean. Although skeptical, the Mexicans listened politely to Frémont's explanation.

Several days later, as Frémont and his men were camping not far from Monterey, a Mexican army officer rode up with orders for him to leave the country immediately. Although the Mexicans were thoroughly within their rights to evict the armed men, Frémont angrily rejected the orders as an insult to him and his country.

To emphasize his defiance, Frémont built a small fort of wooden logs and raised the American flag as his men cheered. They remained there for three days, without any problems, until Frémont decided to withdraw and continue his exploration.

He marched north into Oregon, camping near Klamath Lake. On May 9, a young officer, Lieutenant Archibald H. Gillespie of the Marine Corps, who had left Washington six months before, arrived with messages for Frémont. He carried letters from Frémont's family and an oral report on the deteriorating conditions with Mexico. To this day, no one knows precisely what orders Gillespie carried, but Frémont acted as if he had received instructions to speed back to California with his small army, ready to fight. As he explained later in his memoirs:

The information through Gillespie had absolved me from my duty as an explorer, and I was left to my duty as an officer of the American Army, with the further authoritative knowledge that the Government intended to take California.

Frémont knew that the men under his command, although they were civilians and not soldiers, could be a powerful force if fighting broke out. He made up his mind to use them to conquer California.

For the conquest of California, Polk had dispatched three units. Besides Frémont, they included a naval fleet commanded by Commodore John D. Sloat, with orders to seize California if war broke out. Polk also had ordered the First Dragoons, commanded by General

The Third Expedition: California

Stephen Watts Kearny, in Fort Leavenworth, Kansas, to capture New Mexico and then march on to conquer California.

When Congress declared war against Mexico on May 12, events in California came to a head—even though news of the war did not reach California until much later.

Before they even knew that war had begun, American settlers, worried that they might be ordered out of California by the Mexican government, took action. Without firing a shot, about thirty armed settlers captured a Mexican army post at Sonoma, just north of present-day San Francisco, on June 14. After pulling down the Mexican flag, they raised a different flag, a ragged one made of whitish-brown cloth, with a red star and the image of a brown grizzly bear painted on it, together with the words *California Republic*.

Flag of the short-lived Bear Flag Republic of California

Thus was born what came to be known as the Bear Flag Republic. To justify themselves, the rebels said their purpose was to overthrow a selfish, incompetent government and to guarantee peace and security to all. When they heard that the Mexicans were preparing to take action to put down the revolt, they appealed to Frémont, who was camped at Sutter's Fort, for help.

At the head of his armed civilians, Frémont rode into Sonoma on June 25. Acting on his own initiative, he combined his force with the armed settlers, organizing them into what was called the California-Battalion. It consisted of 234 men in four companies. They were not part of the United States Army although their commander was; they were just armed civilians.

Frémont leading the California Battalion near Monterey

The Third Expedition: California

But a question remained: Who ruled California? The Mexicans, who retained formal title to the province; the rebellious settlers; the newly arrived Americans; or the native Californios?

Again acting boldly, Frémont, with the consent of the settlers, raised the American flag over Sonoma, thus ending the Bear Flag Republic—which had lasted just three short weeks. Luckily for Frémont, events proved him right. Commander Sloat, having received word by ship of the war between Mexico and the United States, captured Monterey, then the capital of California, on July 7. He raised the American flag, claiming the Mexican province for the United States.

Leading the California Battalion, Frémont rode into Monterey shortly thereafter. One observer described him as "a slender and well-proportioned man, of sedate but pleasing countenance . . . His dress . . . was a blue flannel shirt, after the naval style, open at the collar, which was turned over; over this a deerskin hunting shirt, figured and trimmed in hunter's style, blue cloth pantaloons and neat moccasins."

In Monterey, he found that Commodore Sloat, aged and uncertain about his role, had turned command of the United States naval forces over to his assistant, Commodore Robert F. Stockton, an energetic younger officer. Stockton immediately put the California Battalion into the naval service, naming Frémont as its commander. Together, they planned an active campaign to secure California for the United States.

Frémont sailed south to San Diego and captured it. He then marched north to Los Angeles, meeting Stockton there. They entered the city without a fight, ending opposition to American rule of California—for a time.

In August, Stockton organized a civil government for California, naming Frémont as its governor. For Frémont that was an additional honor, as he had also been promoted to the rank of lieutenant colonel in the United States Army.

But his triumph was not to last long.

S I X

Disappointment and Court-Martial

Frémont's life changed dramatically with the arrival in California of General Stephen Watts Kearny and his army of the West.

After taking possession of New Mexico, Kearny had led his troops out of Santa Fe on September 25, 1846, bound for California. On the way, he had met Kit Carson, who was returning to Washington with reports of the conquest of California. Hearing that news, Kearny sent most of his soldiers south to Mexico, but kept about one hundred men to continue on to California, ordering Carson to act as a guide.

When Kearny arrived in southern California, he learned that the conquest of California was far from finished. Some of the local residents—the Californios—had revolted against American rule. With his reduced force, Kearny rashly attacked them at San Pasqual and lost about twenty men. Stockton came to his rescue with a force of sailors

General Stephen Watts Kearny

and marines, and the Californios were defeated outside Los Angeles on January 9, 1847.

The Californios retreated to the north and surrendered to Frémont, who had taken no part in the battle. That ended the military rebellion. The Americans had conquered California.

What followed was a political struggle between the two commanders of the American forces in California, Kearny and Stockton. Each considered himself in charge of the government of California.

Kearny had come with these orders, "Should you conquer or take possession of New Mexico and upper California, or considerable places in either, you will establish temporary civil governments therein." Stockton had similar orders to take and hold all of California and establish a civilian government.

Commodore Robert F. Stockton

Frémont was caught in the middle. He was commander of the California Battalion, which was part of the navy, under the command of Stockton. He also was a lieutenant colonel of the army, subject to the orders of General Kearny.

The issue came to a head on January 16, when Frémont received conflicting instructions. Stockton issued a proclamation appointing a new commander of the California Battalion, and officially promoted Frémont to be governor and commander in chief in California. But Kearny ordered Frémont not to make any changes in the California Battalion.

The next day, Kearny sent for Frémont and asked if he had received his orders. In reply, Frémont handed his superior a letter, which said:

> *I feel myself . . . with great deference to your professional and personal character, constrained to say, that, until you and Commodore Stockton adjust between yourselves the question of rank, where I respectfully think the difficulty belongs, I shall have to report and receive orders, as heretofore from the commodore.*

With that, Frémont made a major mistake. Not only was he disobeying an order from a superior army officer, he also put it in writing.

Kearny restrained his anger. He told Frémont that, as a much older man and a soldier with a warm regard for both Senator Benton and Jessie, he advised Frémont to take back the letter and destroy it.

Frémont refused. His pride and vanity did not permit him to admit that he had made one of the most serious errors a military officer can make—disobeying a lawful command from a superior officer.

The impasse lasted until February, when a new commander of the naval forces, Commodore William Branford Shubrick, arrived, replacing Stockton. Shubrick reversed Stockton's orders. He accepted Kearny as both commander of the armed forces and the civil governor of California.

In March, Kearny ordered Frémont to turn all his documents and papers over to him, and to enlist the California Battalion into the army. Once again, Frémont was reluctant. He rode to Monterey for an interview with Kearny.

Kearny asked him if he would obey the order.

Frémont hesitated. He was torn between his ambition and his duty as an army officer.

Kearny warned him that his answer was very important. "If he wanted to take an hour for consideration, to take it; if he wanted a day for consideration, he could take it."

Frémont left the room. Faced with a difficult situation, he came to the only possible answer for an army officer. He returned in about an hour and said he would obey.

Back in Los Angeles, facing the men of the California Battalion, he asked if they were willing to serve in the army. When they learned that Frémont would no longer be their commander, not one of them agreed. They were discharged from any further military service. With that, Frémont was left with only the nineteen men hired for the original mapping mission of the Topographical Corps under his command.

In May, Kearny felt that his orders had been fulfilled. He had established a civilian government and could safely leave, with one of his senior officers staying behind to govern. He ordered Frémont to come with him when he left California on May 31.

Shortly after their arrival at Fort Leavenworth on August 22, Kearny summoned Frémont to the post headquarters. In a formal written order, he directed him to return all the horses and other public property under his control to officers at the post. He then gave these orders:

Lieutenant Colonel Frémont having performed the above duty will consider himself under arrest and will then repair to Washington City and report himself to the Adjutant General of the Army.

Senator Thomas Hart Benton

Disappointment and Court-Martial

Shocked, Frémont saluted and left. Instead of returning east to his family and the nation as a hero, he was going back to face a military court-martial—a trial—accused of mutiny, disobedience to the lawful commands of a superior officer, and conduct prejudicial to military discipline.

Frémont's court-martial began at noon on November 2, 1847, in the Washington Arsenal. It was a drama of intense interest in the nation's capital. Members of Congress and the press crowded into the large, gloomy trial room to see the clash between the brash young officer, then thirty-four years old, and the stern senior general, fifty-three years old.

Thirteen army officers in colorful dress uniforms decorated with gold braid sat at a long table in front of the room as the jury. Frémont sat calmly at a side table, accompanied by two civilian lawyers—his father-in-law, Senator Benton, and his brother-in-law, William Carey Jones—who, according to army rules, were not permitted to ask questions.

After the charges were read, the trial began. Frémont said his defense would cover two points: one, that he was caught in the middle of the struggle for power between General Kearny and Commodore Stockton, and two, that Kearny was prejudiced against him.

The most dramatic part of the trial followed. Kearny, the star witness for the prosecution, took the witness chair. Frémont began to question him.

Both men were polite as they went over in detail the confusing events in California. For those who were Kearny's supporters, the testimony was clear: Frémont had refused to obey lawful orders. For Frémont supporters, the evidence clearly showed that Kearny had trapped him into an impossible situation.

Newspapers across the country treated the trial as one of the most important news stories of the day. The public seemed fascinated by the personal and political clash between the romantic young officer and the stern older commander.

After weeks of testimony, on January 24, Frémont summed up his defense thusly:

Disappointment and Court-Martial

My acts in California have all been from high motives, and a desire for public service. My scientific labors did something to open California to the knowledge of my countrymen; its geography had been a sealed book. My military operations were conquests without bloodshed; my civil administration was for the public good. I offer California, during my administration, for comparison with the most tranquil portions of the United States . . . I prevented civil war against Governor Stockton, by refusing to join General Kearny against him.

With that plea, the trial ended. After three days of deliberation, the court decided on January 31 that Frémont was guilty on all counts. It sentenced him to be dismissed from the service. The court sent its verdict to President Polk, with a recommendation for leniency because of Frémont's distinguished services. As commander in chief of the army, Polk had the final word on any court-martial decision.

Polk reversed the conviction on the charge of mutiny, but agreed that Frémont had disobeyed a superior officer and that his conduct was prejudicial to military discipline. He accepted the court's recommendation for leniency, rejecting its verdict of dismissal from the service as too harsh and, in written orders, said,

Lieutenant Colonel Frémont will accordingly be released from arrest, will resume his sword, and report for duty.

For Frémont, the verdict was a stunning disappointment. He had expected to be cleared of all wrongdoing. He felt that he could not accept Polk's gesture of leniency, because that would mean admitting his guilt. Declaring his innocence, he resigned from the army.

S E V E N

The fourth Expedition

Instead of being disgraced by the court-martial, Frémont emerged as a hero. The citizens of Charleston presented him with a gold-decorated sword. The Prussian government and the Royal Geographical Society in Great Britain gave him gold medals. Magazines and newspapers praised his explorations.

And several businessmen in St. Louis called upon him to make another expedition, seeking a new central route suitable for a railroad to the Pacific. That fit in perfectly with Frémont's plans for his own future.

Years earlier, on his first visit to California, he had been so impressed by its "delightful climate and uncommon beauty" that he determined to make his home there. He had asked Thomas Larkin, the consul at Monterey, to buy a ranch for him, and Larkin had done so—purchasing a 70-square-mile tract called Las Mariposas, covering 43,000 acres (17,400 hectares) in the foothills of the Sierrra Nevada Mountains.

The Sierra Nevada Mountains

Planning for a return to California, he knew that the chief obstacles to a railroad line were the heavy snows that blocked passage over the mountains in winter. As he had in the past, Frémont considered this to be a challenge—he would find a way through the snowcapped mountains.

His fourth expedition began on October 21, 1848, when he led a party of thirty-three men on horseback out of Westport Landing. A month later, they arrived at Pueblo, a small settlement in Colorado, where they were warned about the exceptionally heavy snow that year.

Ignoring the warnings, the Frémont party pushed ahead into the mountains, through blizzards, snow, ice, and sleet. It was slow going. The men suffered from frozen toes, hands, and ears. As the temperatures frequently dropped below zero, their pack mules, carrying food, began to drop one by one, dying on the trail.

The Fourth Expedition

On December 11, they reached the banks of the Rio Grande, which was frozen solid. In front of them was the main range of the lofty Rocky Mountains, with peaks as high as 14,000 feet (4,267 meters) above sea level. Despite the obvious suffering of the men and animals, Frémont decided to go on, to find a pass by which he could cross the mountains.

It was the wrong decision, resulting in disaster—suffering, starvation, and death.

For days, the men struggled through snowdrifts and bone-chilling cold wind. Their mules, ravenous with hunger, began to eat leather ropes, even gnawing at the leather saddles. Finally, Frémont was forced to admit defeat and ordered their retreat.

But things got worse as they moved back. On New Year's Day, 1849, their supply of mules, killed for meat, ran out. There was nothing left to eat.

Frémont sent out a party of four strong men to bring back relief, while the rest of the expedition slowly retraced its steps. When the party did not return, Frémont himself and a few others started back to seek help. One by one, the men began to drop. Eleven died of starvation and cold.

Looking like "walking skeletons," the twenty-two survivors made it to Kit Carson's ranch near Taos, New Mexico, where they recovered. Even though some blamed Frémont for the disaster, others still had faith in him. Determined to complete his mission, he recruited twenty-five men, including some who had suffered in the mountains. After a short rest, they set out once more for California.

This time, he took a more prudent route, avoiding the Rocky Mountains by going across the Mexican border, north to Tucson in Arizona, and then west along the Gila River. The weather was pleasant in the spring, and the expedition met no obstacles.

As Frémont moved along the Gila River, he saw in the distance a huge crowd of dust. He quickly rode up and discovered a large number of Mexican men, women, and children—later estimated to be about twelve hundred people—with mules pulling carts and horses loaded with packs.

JOHN AUGUSTUS SUTTER

John Augustus Sutter (1803–1880) became famous in 1848 when gold was discovered on his land on the American River about fifty miles northwest of Sacramento. That started the "gold rush" of fortune-seekers to California in 1849. These fortune-seekers were called "the forty-niners."

Sutter, who was born in Switzerland, came to California in 1839 and started a cattle ranch. He built his headquarters in the form of a fort, protected by cannon. It became known as Sutter's Fort. He was a gracious host to the many weary and hungry travelers who came through the snowy Sierra Nevada.

Sutter did not become rich as a result of the discovery of gold, but rather the victim of thousands of newcomers who invaded his property. In less than a year, he sold the fort and retired to a nearby farm. He died in 1880 at the age of seventy-six.

Today, a restored Sutter's Fort stands in California as a state historic site.

John Augustus Sutter

The Fourth Expedition

"Where are you going?" Frémont asked.

"California."

"Why so many of you?"

"Gold! Gold!" came the answer.

It was the first news that Frémont received of the discovery of gold in California. It was the beginning of what came to be known as "the Gold Rush of 1849," when thousands of Americans and others flocked into California to get rich quickly.

For Frémont, it was good news. If gold had been discovered at Sutter's ranch, why couldn't there be gold at his new ranch? Acting on that belief, he quickly hired twenty-eight of the Mexicans to pan for gold on his land, with the proceeds to be divided equally. The Mexicans joined his expedition, and it sped into California.

Gold *was* discovered on the Frémont ranch, and he—and the Mexicans he had hired—became rich.

The California Gold Rush sparked a huge wave of emigration to the west. Most hopeful emigrants traveled by wagon train through rough terrain.

ϵ I G H T

The Fifth Expedition

By 1850, at the age of thirty-seven, Frémont had reached the peak of success. He had a loving wife and children, wealth, a successful ranch, and a reputation as the foremost explorer of the West—and he was one of the leading citizens of California.

With California's population growing rapidly, swollen by the rush of the "forty-niners" to the gold fields, its people moved for admission to the Union as a state. In November 1849, California adopted a state constitution. A month later, the state legislature met in San Jose to elect its first two senators.

The major issue of the day in California and the United States was slavery, with the country divided between pro- and antislavery advocates. Although he was from the South, where slavery was protected by law, Frémont strongly opposed the extension of slavery to new states.

The California legislature avoided the issue by electing one senator

San Francisco became a booming city after the Gold Rush and Frémont's influence.

from each faction—Frémont, the antislavery man, and William M. Gwin, a proslavery advocate.

Frémont took his seat as one of the first two senators from California when it was admitted to the Union as the thirty-first state on September 9, 1850. But his term as senator lasted only until March 1851, ending when the Senate adjourned. Frémont returned to problems.

The title to his ranch was in question, mainly due to differences between Mexican and American law. More immediately, his political future was in doubt. When his first term expired, he ran for re-election, but was defeated because proslavery forces had gained a majority in the California legislature.

After a brief vacation tour of Europe, Frémont returned to the United States in 1853, prepared to take part once again in exploring a possible route for a railroad line to the Pacific. Washington officials had designated five different paths for exploration with army officers in command—leaving no room for Frémont despite his vast experience.

With the backing of Senator Benton, Frémont decided he would find a suitable route on his own, without any official status. "He proposes to start in November and thus to test the practicality of the route during the seasons of snows," a St. Louis newspaper, the *Democrat*, reported.

The Fifth Expedition

Frémont's fifth and last expedition crossed Kansas, and arrived at Bent's Fort in Colorado on November 30. It was easy moving west through the Cochetopa Pass, more than 10,000 feet (3,050 meters) in elevation, on the Continental Divide. In mid-December, Frémont found only four inches of snow on the ground, which indicated that it was a possible path for a railroad over the mountains.

But as the expedition moved farther west, the expedition ran into trouble. Cold and weary, the men stumbled up steep mountains and through icy streams. Running out of food in the southwest corner of Utah, they killed some of their horses and mules and ate them.

Despite the tall mountain ranges looming before them, the relentless cold, and the dwindling food supply, Frémont demonstrated his skill and leadership. Confidently, he pulled out his pocket compass and led his men forward. One of them, Alexis Godey, later wrote in praise of Frémont's "daring energy, his indomitable perseverance, and his goodness of heart."

Their food supply ran out. For forty-eight hours the men had nothing at all to eat, but still they pushed on.

Finally, on February 8, 1854, they straggled into the tiny Mormon community of Parowan, in the southwest corner of Utah. The hospitable Mormons offered shelter and food for the starving men, who stayed there almost two weeks recovering.

The rest of the trip was comparatively easy. Frémont left on February 21, and crossed Nevada into California, where he found his path blocked by snow in the Sierra Nevada. He turned south to avoid the mountains, and without difficulty reached the San Joaquin Valley, where the wildflowers had begun to bloom. Frémont arrived in San Francisco in April 1854, almost six months after he had started.

Although the precise routes that he had traveled were not used, Frémont's findings were useful to the later builders of the first transcontinental railroad, which was completed many years later, in 1869.

N I N E

Presidential Candidate

"Free Soil, Free Speech, Free Men, Frémont."

That was the slogan of the new Republican Party in 1856, when it nominated Frémont as its first candidate for president.

Frémont's nomination came at a time when the United States was deeply divided over the issue of slavery. In the South, slavery was legal and accepted, but elsewhere in the country the movement for abolition of slavery was growing. The issue reached a crucial point when Southerners insisted that slavery should be permitted in new states admitted to the Union, while Northerners opposed any extension of slavery beyond the South.

As the election of 1856 drew closer, leaders of the Democratic Party approached Frémont, who was a lifelong Democrat, to offer him its nomination for president. He had the credentials of a good candidate: youth (he was forty-three years old); fame (because of his exploits as an

A Republican campaign poster, 1856

explorer); an attractive family (his wife, Jessie, and their three living children); and a reputation as a leader (he had been governor of California briefly, and a United States senator).

The Democrats had conditions, though. Frémont had to endorse both the Fugitive Slave Law, which made it a crime not to return fleeing slaves to their owners, and the Kansas-Nebraska Act, which had created the Kansas and Nebraska territories and allowed the people in the territories to vote on whether or not to permit slavery. For Frémont, who had been an opponent of slavery all his life despite his Southern birth, these were impossible conditions. He refused the offer.

Surprisingly, that did not end his political life. The leaders of the just-organized Republican Party turned to him, mainly because he was a new face on the Washington scene, untouched by the bitter Congressional fights between pro- and anti-slavery forces.

When the Republican Party's first convention opened on June 17, 1856, in Philadelphia, it nominated Frémont on a platform opposing the extension of slavery to the territories. The Democrats nominated James

Buchanan of Pennsylvania, described by a Richmond, Virginia, newspaper as a man who "had never uttered a word that could pain the most sensitive Southern heart."

Thus, the issue in the 1856 presidential campaign was simple and clear; Frémont opposed slavery, Buchanan did not. The Democrats warned that if Frémont won, the South would secede and the United States would fall apart. The Republicans argued that, although there should not be any interference with slavery in the South, its expansion should end.

It turned out to be a dirty, hard-fought campaign. In those days before radio, television, and polls, both candidates stayed at home. They did not make campaign appearances or speeches, but their supporters did—in torchlight parades, mass meetings, rallies, and picnics.

Many false charges against Frémont were raised during the campaign, including that he was a hard drinker, a slaveholder, foreign-born, a crook, and a Catholic (religious prejudice against Catholics was strong at the time). Frémont, who was an Episcopalian, refused to dignify the scurrilous charges by publicly denying them.

He said the main issue of the campaign was freedom, including religious freedom, and under the Constitution there were no religious tests for office holding. He was right, of course, but his principled stance cost him some votes.

Frémont lost. He got 1,321,264 popular votes, carrying eleven states with 114 electoral votes. Buchanan received 1,838,169 votes, winning nineteen states with 174 electoral votes.

Disappointed, Frémont returned to private life. He had lost, but he had energized the new Republican Party and set the stage for the election of Abraham Lincoln four years later.

T E N

The Civil War

Frémont and his wife were traveling in Europe in 1861 when they heard about the start of the Civil War. They rushed back home to Washington, where Frémont offered his services to President Lincoln.

Frémont had imposing credentials—a vast knowledge of the West, service as an army officer, a sterling antislavery record, a reputation as a hero for his many expeditions to California—and he had been the first Republican candidate for president.

Recognizing the importance of retaining control of the Mississippi Valley, Lincoln named Frémont a major general to command the area. His mission was to ensure Union control of Missouri, the upper Mississippi Valley, and the vast area between the Mississippi and the Rocky Mountains.

President Abraham Lincoln

When Frémont arrived at his headquarters in St. Louis in July 1861, he found a hostile city. Jessie Frémont described the scene:

> *Steamboats stood idly at their wharves, the streets were practically deserted, a Confederate flag flew from secessionist headquarters, and business houses stood gloomily behind their iron shutters.*

Not only was Southern sentiment strong in Missouri, but also with Confederate armies nearby threatening to advance, Frémont found himself short of arms, ammunition, and soldiers.

Frémont threw himself into what seemed to be an impossible task. He worked at his headquarters from five o'clock in the morning until midnight, trying to prepare his forces for the coming battles.

Frémont's record as a general was mixed. He accomplished much. He stopped the open recruiting of Confederate forces, he reorganized the reserve corps, and he reinforced the defenses of St. Louis. But with limited resources, he was unable to send reinforcements to two armies in the field, and they both suffered defeats.

His greatest difficulty came in dealing with the Blair family of Missouri, which had originally been among his strongest supporters. Montgomery Blair was in Washington, a member of Lincoln's cabinet. In St. Louis, his brother Frank Blair attempted to get his friends contracts to supply the army, as well as a commission as a major general for himself. When Frémont resisted his demands, the Blairs became enemies and sought his dismissal.

Frémont faced major military problems, too. By the end of August 1861, rebel guerrillas had created a perilous situation for civilians all over Missouri. They raided farms, burned bridges, wrecked railroad trains, cut telegraph lines, and drove countless families to flee.

Faced with developing chaos, Frémont took decisive action. On August 30, he issued a proclamation declaring Missouri to be under martial law, ordering that:

> *The property, real and personal, of all persons in the state of Mis-*
> *souri who shall take up arms against the United States, or who shall*
> *be directly proven to have taken an active part with their enemies in*
> *the field, is declared confiscated to the public use, and their slaves, if*
> *any they have, are hereby declared freemen.*

For Lincoln, Frémont's proclamation was a major error that could endanger Union sentiment in the border states. Up to that point, Lincoln had justified the war as a means to preserve the Union, but Frémont's declaration added a controversial new dimension—freeing the slaves. Lincoln was not ready to do that. His own Emancipation Proclamation was more than a year off (it wasn't issued until January 1, 1863). Lincoln requested that Frémont withdraw his proclamation, and he did. But Lincoln had lost confidence in him, and relieved him of his command on November 2, 1861.

That did not end the controversy, though. Frémont had strong supporters among the vocal antislavery advocates in the North. One example was a poem written by John Greenleaf Whittier that included these lines:

> *Thy error, Frémont, was to act*
> *A brave man's part, without the statesman's tact*

Under considerable political pressure, Lincoln found another post for Frémont. In March 1862, he appointed him to command an army operating in western Virginia, Kentucky, and Tennessee.

Once again, Frémont was placed in an impossible situation, with orders to advance but without adequate arms, ammunition, and supplies. Like many other Union commanders, Frémont was defeated by the brilliant Southern general Stonewall Jackson. Lincoln reacted by consolidating the Union forces in the area, including Frémont's, under another general. Frémont asked to be relieved of his command.

ELEVEN

Aftermath

When Frémont resigned his commission as a major general in 1864, his active public career came to an end. At the age of fifty-one, he returned to private life.

From then until his death, he experienced a series of failures. His ranch at Mariposa, which had made him a millionaire, turned into a financial loss, largely because of the untrustworthy men he had hired to run it while he was gone. He took his remaining money and put it into a planned railroad from Kansas to California, but it, too, failed, and he became penniless.

For a while, Frémont and his wife lived in New York City, supported by Jessie's earnings as a freelance writer of articles for magazines. Friends in Washington came to his rescue, and President Rutherford B. Hayes appointed him governor of the territory of Arizona in 1878.

Frémont apparently enjoyed his duties as territorial governor, but his

John Charles Frémont, following his court-martial.

wife's ill health caused her to return to New York. Frémont resigned in 1883 to join her back East. As Jessie continued to write, Frémont decided that he, too, would write, and he began with the story of his life.

The book, entitled *Memoirs of My Life: A Retrospect of Fifty Years*, was published in 1887.

A large book—650 pages long—it did not sell very well, and did nothing to ease the Frémonts' financial problems.

In April 1890, Congress belatedly recognized his contributions by restoring to him the rank of major general in the army, retired, with a pension of $6,000 a year, which was a sizable income then. For the first time since the end of the Civil War, the Frémonts appeared to be financially secure.

But his life did not last long after that. Frémont came down with a serious illness later that year, and on July 13, 1890, died in New York City at the age of seventy-seven. His wife died in 1902.

Today, John Charles Frémont is one of the forgotten men in American history. But he should be remembered for his major achievements as an explorer of the West, who found and marked the paths through the plains, mountains, and deserts that thousands of American settlers followed in their migrations from the Mississippi River to the Pacific Ocean. Historian Allan Nevins said, "His one great definite and tangible contribution to American life was his geographical work, and as long as the early history of the Great West lives, his name will live with it."

His wife, Jessie, put it more dramatically. "From the ashes of his campfires have sprung cities."

FRÉMONT AND HIS TIMES

1813   Born on January 21 in Charleston, South Carolina

1829-1831   Attends Charleston College

1833   Appointed second lieutenant in the Topographical Corps of the army

1836-1837   Explores Cherokee region of Georgia

1841   Maps Iowa territory; marries Jessie Benton

1842   First expedition. Explores South Pass and the Wind River Range

1843   Publishes *Narrative of the Exploring Expedition to the Rocky Mountains*

1843–1844   Second expedition. Explores routes to Oregon, Washington, and California

1845–1846   Third expedition. Explores central Rocky Mountains and California

1847   Appointed governor of California

1847–1848   Court-martialed for mutiny; convicted, resigns from army

1848–1849   Fourth expedition. Seeks route for railroad line to the Pacific

1850   Elected senator from California

1853–1854   Fifth expedition. Seeks southern route for railroad line to California

1856   Nominated as first Republican candidate for president; loses election

1861   Appointed Union army major general in Missouri during Civil War

1862   Appointed to command a Union army in western Virginia

1878   Appointed governor of the Arizona Territory

1887   *Memoirs of My Life: A Retrospect of Fifty Years* published

1890   Dies on July 13 in New York City, at age seventy-seven

Source Notes

Chapter 1

8 "Of middle size . . ." Smith, Fredrika Shumway, *Frémont: Soldier, Explorer, Statesman.* (Rand, McNally, 1966), p. 12.

8 "At sixteen . . ." Frémont, John Charles, *Memoirs of My Life: A Retrospect of Fifty Years.* (Belford, Clarke & Company 1887), p. 18.

8 "Habitual regularity . . ." Nevins, Allan, *Frémont: Pathmarker of the West,* (D. Appleton Century Company, 1939), p. 26.

8 "I smiled . . ." *Memoirs,* p. 19.

11 "Here I found . . ." *Memoirs,* p. 24.

Chapter 2

15 "At length . . ." *Memoirs,* p. 24.

16 "This was . . ." *Memoirs,* p. 41.

17 "A steamboat . . ." *Memoirs,* p. 54.

17 "First the foundations . . ." *Memoirs,* p. 64.

19 "There came a glow . . ." *Memoirs,* p. 67.

Chapter 3

26 "No one was . . ." Nevins, p. 99.

30 "sprang on . . ." *Memoirs,* p. 150.

31 "This flag was raised . . ." Nevins, p. 116.

Chapter 4

32 "Only trust me . . ." Egan, p. 131.

36 "The snow deepened . . ." *Memoirs,* p. 326.

38 "We now considered . . ." *Memoirs,* p. 338.

39 "Desolate and revolting..." Frémont, p. 389.

Chapter 5

42 "The beginning of two crowded years . . ." Nevins, p. 428.

44 "The information . . ." *Memoirs,* p. 448.

47 "A slender . . ." Smith, p. 150.

Chapter 6

50 "Should you conquer . . ." Nevins, p. 309.

51 "I feel myself . . ." Egan, p. 411.

52 "If he wanted . . ." Transcript of Frémont's Court Martial, p. 104

52 "Lieutenant Colonel Frémont . . ." Clarke, Dwight L., *Stephen Watts Kearny: Soldier of the West*. (University of Oklahoma Press, 1961), p. 335.

55 "My acts in California . . ." Transcript, p. 446.

55 "Lieutenant Colonel Frémont . . ." Johnson, Kenneth M. *The Frémont Court Martial*. (Dawson's Book Shop, 1968), p. 76.

Chapter 7
56 "Delightful climate . . ." *Memoirs*, p. 419.

58 "Walking skeletons . . ." Nevins, p. 365.

60 "Where are you going?" Nevins, p. 373.

Chapter 8
62 "He proposes . . ." Nevins, p. 410.

63 "Daring energy . . ." Nevins, p. 416.

Chapter 9
64 "Free soil . . ." Boller, Paul F. Jr., *Presidential Campaigns*. (Oxford University Press, 1996), p. 92.

67 "Had never uttered . . ." Boller, p. 92.

Chapter 10
70 "Steamboats stood . . ." Egan, p. 514.

70 "The property . . ." Egan, p. 515.

71 "Thy error . . ." Smith, p. 226.

Chapter 11
73 "His one great . . ." Nevins, p. 621.

73 "From his ashes . . ." Nevins, p. 616.

Further Research

Books:

Faber, Harold. *From Sea to Sea: The Growth of the United States*. New York: Scribner, 1992.

Faber, Harold. *The Discoverers of America*. New York: Scribner, 1992.

Lomask, Milton. *Great Lives: Exploration*. New York: Scribner, 1988.

Smith, Fredrika Shumway. *Frémont: Soldier, Explorer, Statesman*. Chicago: Rand, McNally, 1966.

Websites:

The Oregon Trail

www.themaphouse.com/millencat/usa4545.html

Major General John C. Frémont

www.longcamp.com

Bibliography

Benton, Thomas Hart. *Thirty Years' View; or, A History of the Working of the American Government for Thirty Years From 1820 to 1850*. New York: D. Appleton, 1886.

De Voto, Bernard. *The Course of Empire*. Norwalk, CT: Easton Press, 1988.

Egan, Ferol. *Frémont: Explorer for a Restless Nation*. Garden City: Doubleday, 1977

Faber, Harold. *From Sea to Sea: The Growth of the United States*. New York: Scribner, 1992.

Faber, Harold. *The Discoverers of America*. New York: Scribners, 1992.

Frémont, John Charles. *Narrative of the Exploring Expedition to the Rocky Mountains, in the Year 1842*. Syracuse: Hall & Dickson, 1848.

Frémont, John Charles. *The Exploring Expedition to the Rocky Mountains, Oregon and California*. Buffalo: G.H. Derby, 1849.

Frémont, John Charles. *Memoirs of My Life: A Retrospect of Fifty Years*. Chicago: Belford, Clarke & Company, 1887.

Marcy, William Learned. *The Proceedings of the Court Martial in the Trial of Lieutenant Colonel Frémont*. Washington: 30th Congress, 1848.

INDEX

Page numbers in **boldface** are illustrations.